Editor:
Janet Cain, M.Ed..

Editorial Project Manager:
Ina Massler Levin, M.A.

Editor in Chief:
Sharon Coan, M.S. Ed.

Art Director:
Elayne Roberts

Associate Designer:
Denise Bauer

Cover Artists:
Sue Fullam
Jose L. Tapia

Product Manager:
Phil Garcia

Imaging:
James Edward Grace

Publishers:
Rachelle Cracchiolo, M.S. Ed.
Mary Dupuy Smith, M.S. Ed.

Grades 2-5

How to Write a Sentence

Author:

Kathleen Christopher Null

Teacher Created Materials, Inc.
P.O. Box 1040
Huntington Beach, CA 92647
ISBN-1-55734-326-7

©1997 Teacher Created Materials, Inc.   Made in U.S.A.

Table of Contents

Introduction

This book will enable you to teach students the basics of sentence writing in an enjoyable and memorable fashion. The first section, *This Is a Sentence!* (pages 6–9), provides a foundation for the activities in the sections which follow. Each page in this section provides basic information about sentences which you may pass on to your students in whatever manner best suits their abilities and needs. If they have already been taught the basics, you may wish to have them read the pages and do the activities independently. In such a case, you may find it advantageous to reproduce selected answers from the *Answer Key* (pages 46–48) and make them available to students so the activities become self-checking. Expand on the activities and instruction if your students are having difficulty with a particular concept, or simply choose only those activities that are needed to enrich learning. *What Is a Sentence?* (page 6) and *Are You a Good Sentence Detective?* (page 7) familiarize students with the basic components required in each sentence and allow them to strengthen that knowledge by distinguishing sentences from nonsentences. *Sentence Emergencies!* (page 8) gives students the opportunity to be "emergency sentence technicians" as they practice their editing skills. *What Do You Think?* (page 9) introduces them to the concept of complete sentences in an activity that will prepare them for the next section of this book.

Let's Hear It for Complete Sentences! (pages 10–13) is the second section. It contains four activities that will help students hone their abilities to recognize and write complete sentences. *Whoa!* (page 10) is the first activity. It introduces run-on sentences and explains how to rein them in. *Finding Hidden Sentences* (page 11) gives students a new challenge. They will find sentences that are hidden within a block of text. *Bits and Pieces* (page 12) introduces sentence fragments, and *Fragment Search* (page 13) can be used to expand this concept.

The third section is *Don't Forget to Punctuate and Capitalize!* (pages 14–16). It includes three activities to teach and reinforce the correct use of capitalization and punctuation. First you will find *That's Capital!* (page 14), an activity that gives students a chance to practice capitalization rules. *End Marks* (page 15) covers punctuation marks that go at the ends of sentences. This section concludes with *Punctuation Rules* (page 16), which presents additional punctuation rules and provides a reinforcement activity for the students. While this page does not cover all punctuation rules, it is an extension of the basics that have already been covered in this book. Since learning these punctuation rules is more challenging, this activity is most appropriate for older or more advanced students. It can also be modified for students learning beginning punctuation if you take the time to go over how the types of punctuation shown can be used in a variety of ways. It might be useful to create a poster or chart listing the rules for various punctuation marks and showing examples of each for student reference.

Introduction *(cont.)*

The Subject: A V.I.P. (pages 17–19) is the title of the fourth section. The subject is a very important part of speech. *What Is a Subject?* (page 17) and *Subject Practice* (page 18) provide useful information and activities about what a subject is, how to recognize it, and how to use a subject in a sentence. *Very Important Subjects* (page 19) is an activity that allows students to do some creative writing using the sentence components they have learned thus far. This activity also provides a brief introduction to predicates which are covered in the next section.

The fifth section is *The Predicate: Another V.I.P.* (pages 20–23). It contains everything you will need to teach your students the role of the predicate in a sentence. The first activity, *What Is a Predicate?* (page 20) focuses on the predicate itself by introducing the role of the predicate in a sentence. The last two activities in this section, *What Is Missing?* (page 21) and *Matching* (pages 22 and 23), give the opportunity to write and match subject/predicate pairs. Simply reproduce the cards on stu or cardstock and cut them apart. To improve their durability, the cards can be laminated or c with contact paper.

The Verb: The Active V.I.P. (pages 24-28) has a variety of fun-filled activities. It begins with *T is Superb!* (page 24) to provide basic information about verbs. It includes an introductory act. form of a quiz. Students should be encouraged to make their best guesses on this informal Then they should be allowed to check their own answers. They may be surprised to see ho cy get right. Quizzing prior to providing instruction can validate what students already know them focus on the learning that is about to take place. As an alternative, you may wish to iz to reinforce their learning after students have completed the unit on verbs. The quiz is followed by three activities that address action verbs, non–action verbs, and helping verbs. These are entitled *Take Action!*, *Take a Break!*, and *We're Here to Help!* (pages 25–27). The section concludes with *Just One or More?* (page 28). This explains subject-verb agreement and gives students a practice exercise.

The seventh section, *Four Kinds of Sentences* (pages 29–31), is a little different from other sections in that it contains information and examples of declarative, interrogative, imperative, and exclamatory sentences in an easy-to-understand format. The section concludes with *Can You Handle This?* (page 31), an activity that gives students the opportunity to utilize their knowledge and understanding of the four kinds of sentences.

Adding Complements (pages 32–34) follows and is a section devoted to the details that add the finishing touches to make a good and interesting sentence. The first activity, *My Complements to This Sentence!* (page 32), teaches students about sentence complements. The second activity, *Enchanted Enhancements* (pages 33 and 34), enables students to see the differences between a basic sentence and a sentence that has been enhanced by descriptive language.

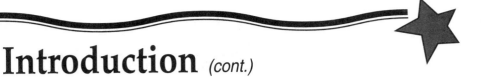

Introduction *(cont.)*

The final section, *Time for Fun* (pages 35–45), rewards students for learning about sentences. It also reinforces everything they have learned about sentence writing. The section includes five activities or games, after which you can use the award page so you can recognize the effort and progress your students have made. *Word Muncher* (page 35) and *Crazy, Mixed-Up Sentences* (page 36) can be done by individual students or teams. In addition, you may expand the *Crazy, Mixed-Up Sentences* activity by using it as a springboard for inspiring students to write stories. The game, *Sentence Construction Teams* (pages 39–41), is played in cooperative learning groups. This game allows for plenty of creativity and surprises. You may wish to expand this into creative writing projects for teams or individuals. *Sentence Maze* (page 42) is an activity that will prove useful when you need to work with individual students. *Sentence Rummy* (pages 43 and 44) is a sentence card game that can be used at any time for fun and reinforcement.

Each of the activities in this book may be used at whatever level is best for your students. Younger or less experienced students will need more guidance and reinforcement. Older or more capable students may work independently much of the time. Many of the activities may be used more than once. For instance, you may wish to reproduce the *Answer Key* (pages 46–48) and attach the appropriate part to the back of an activity or have laminated copies available for self-checking. While some activities are fairly simple and straightforward, others are more challenging. Students may learn more if they are able to self-check, make revisions, and self-check again. This method will prove especially helpful over time, as students' skills improve. Children do not learn merely by taking in all the pertinent information and then immediately applying it. They learn one step at a time through a variety of experiences.

When appropriate, the *Answer Key* shows a piece of writing in correct paragraph form. Since the emphasis of this book is on writing sentences, students are not required to put their written responses into paragraphs. However, many of them will be ready to do so. These students will be able to check their paragraphs as well as their sentences. Students who are not yet ready to write using paragraphs will still be exposed to paragraph form when they check their own answers.

As with all the activities, self-checking is another useful tool for teachers to help students learn. In some cases, you will prefer to check the work with individual students or with the whole class, reviewing and reinforcing new concepts.

This book has been designed to support you and your method of teaching writing. It is intended to be a versatile tool that can be used as you see fit.

What Is a Sentence?

- A sentence begins with a capital letter and ends with a period (.), a question mark (?), or an exclamation point (!).

- A sentence can be a group of words that tells us something.

   Examples: Jacob went to the beach.

   I won first prize!

- A sentence can also be a group of words that asks us a question.

   Example: When did Nancy leave?

- A sentence is always a complete thought.

Circle the sentences below. Remember that each sentence must start with a capital letter; end with a period, question mark, or exclamation point; and be a complete thought.

1. over the rainbow!
2. Becky writes a letter.
3. Does Jaime want?
4. strawberries and bananas
5. Watch out for the ball!
6. when school over?
7. I am in the pool.
8. When Derek

9. Do you like dogs?
10. I can see you!
11. If I stop
12. a house on the hill.
13. why don't you
14. I painted my brother green.
15. It made my mom laugh.

Now write three sentences of your own. End one with a period, one with a question mark, and one with an exclamation point.

1. _____

_____

_____

2. _____

_____

_____

3. _____

_____

_____

Are You a Good Sentence Detective?

A sentence is a group of words that tells us something or asks us a question. It is always a complete thought.

Example: John cooks dinner.

    This is what the sentence tells us.

        It tells us who it is about. *John*

        It tells us what John does. *cooks dinner*

There are only ten complete sentences shown in the magnifying glass. Write these ten sentences on the lines below.

> I'm going swimming after school!
> Tuesday.
> Chris opens the door.
> April
> Will we go to the store tomorrow?
> paper bag
> My iguana ate my homework.
> Juanita helps me.
> Can you come with me?
> the lights!
> My best friend
> Maria dances every day.
> I have a cat.
> That bicycle looks brand new!
> Do you like candy?

1. _____
2. _____
3. _____
4. _____
5. _____
6. _____
7. _____
8. _____
9. _____
10. _____

Sentence Emergencies!

These sentences need your help. Be a sentence doctor and make these sentences better. Rewrite the sentences correctly. Put a capital letter at the beginning of each sentence. Use a period, question mark, or exclamation point at the end of each sentence.

1. tuesday is the day we go to the library

   _____

2. who is your teacher

   _____

3. the students in my class were reading

   _____

4. what a wonderful day it is

   _____

5. jordan, come play with us

   _____

6. watch out, Michelle

   _____

7. do you like math

   _____

8. i will paint today

   _____

9. what time is lunch

   _____

10. i got a sticker

    _____

What Do You Think?

You have learned that every sentence must begin with a capital letter and end with a period, question mark, or exclamation point. You have also learned that a sentence must be a complete thought. A sentence needs to have enough information to make sense. It needs to ask you a complete question or tell you a complete idea. There are ten incomplete sentences on this page. Rewrite sentences to make them complete.

1. Jennifer wants to

_____

2. Yesterday, while it was raining, I

_____

3. Do you

_____

4. all the way down the hill

_____

5. is very annoying

_____

6. I wish I had

_____

7. Did they try

_____

8. Watch out for the

_____

9. is a big, scary monster

_____

10. jumped into the spaghetti

_____

Whoa!

You have learned that each sentence is a complete thought. What about sentences that do not stop when they should? A sentence that runs on to the next thought is called a run-on sentence.

Example:

Cake is the best dessert chocolate is my favorite flavor.
Cake is the best dessert. Chocolate is my favorite flavor.

Each of the following sentences is a run-on sentence. Write each run-on sentence as two separate sentences. The first one has been done for you.

1. My books are on the table my math book is on top.
   My books are on the table. My math book is on top.

2. They were closing the store it was time to go home.

   _____

   _____

3. Watch out for the slippery ice you could fall and hurt yourself.

   _____

   _____

4. I got a new blue dress the blue shoes match perfectly.

   _____

   _____

5. My brother made the team will I be able to play baseball some day?

   _____

   _____

6. I like to go camping the last time we went, we saw a bear.

   _____

   _____

7. My teacher was not at school we had a substitute.

   _____

   _____

8. I don't like lima beans I only want mashed potatoes.

   _____

   _____

9. Can you spend the night at my house we can have pizza for dinner.

   _____

   _____

10. My dog has fleas we had to get her some special medicine.

   _____

   _____

Finding Hidden Sentences

In the paragraphs below you will find ten hidden sentences. See if you can find all of them. Write the ten sentences on the lines. Remember to capitalize and punctuate them.

every day the ice cream truck comes down our street it comes after school and in the summer when I hear the music playing, I run outside sometimes I get to buy some ice cream do you like ice cream

my sister does not like ice cream i think that is crazy how can someone not like ice cream it is nice to eat on a hot summer day i think i like chocolate best of all

1. _____

_____

2. _____

_____

3. _____

_____

4. _____

_____

5. _____

_____

6. _____

_____

7. _____

_____

8. _____

_____

9. _____

_____

10. _____

_____

Bits and Pieces

You have learned that a sentence needs to be a complete thought to make sense. When a sentence is an incomplete thought, it is called a sentence fragment. Usually, a sentence fragment is missing a piece of information. You might not know the subject. The subject tells who or what the sentence is about. You might not know the predicate. The predicate tells what the subject has, does, or is.

Read the sentence fragments shown below. They are missing important pieces of information. Use your imagination to change these fragments into complete sentences. Rewrite the fragments as complete sentences, adding whatever information you wish. The first is done for you. Remember to capitalize and punctuate every sentence.

1. The big bad wolf
   The big bad wolf blew down the little pig's house.

2. went flying in the air

   _____

3. my best friend

   _____

4. Alan's birthday party

   _____

5. fell off the fence

   _____

6. was blowing big bubbles

   _____

7. a giant spider

   _____

8. ran into the street

   _____

9. her hamster

   _____

10. ate a bug

   _____

Fragment Search

On this page, you will find five complete sentences and five sentence fragments. Write the five complete sentences using correct capitalization and punctuation. Use your own words to change the five sentence fragments into complete sentences. Be sure to write these new sentences using correct capitalization and punctuation. You should have written ten complete sentences when you are finished.

1. bruce has many things in his room

   _____

2. books on shelves

   _____

3. is there a box of toys under the bed

   _____

4. a rug is in front of the closet

   _____

5. two stuffed animals

   _____

6. i can see trees from my window

   _____

7. the bedspread and curtains

   _____

8. my favorite game

   _____

9. look out for

   _____

10. latoya cleans her room every day

   _____

That's Capital!

Some words need to be capitalized. This means they start with capital letters.

You should always capitalize
- the first word in a sentence. **Example:** *We* close the windows when it rains.
- the word I. **Examples:** When *I* went to the park, *I* climbed a tree.
- the special names of people and places. **Examples:** *Carl, France, Empire State Building*
- titles of people. **Examples:** *Dr.* Martin, *Mrs.* Garcia, *President* Washington
- titles or family names when they are used in place of a person's name. **Examples:** Good morning, *General*. I saw *Grandpa*. Give the list to *Mom*.
- the days of the week and months of the year. **Examples:** *Monday, Tuesday, Wednesday; January, February, March*
- titles of books, movies, songs, plays, musicals, magazines, newspapers, and television shows.
- school subjects, when they are the names of languages or subject titles. **Examples:** *English, French, Modern Art in America*
- holidays. **Examples:** *Martin Luther King, Jr., Day; Thanksgiving*

The following sentences have some words that need to be capitalized. Cross out each letter that needs to be changed to a capital. Write the capital above the crossed out letter. The first letter is done for you.

W
1. When i went to the store, i saw my teacher, mrs. roe, buying strawberries.

2. my family will go to disneyland in july.

3. i am reading *old yeller* this week.

4. my sister, sarah, says her favorite subject is spanish.

5. on wednesday, we will celebrate groundhog day.

6. my brother said that mom was a cheerleader at roosevelt high school.

7. in august, we're going to visit aunt margaret in san francisco, california.

8. benjie, my little brother, had a birthday and we sang, "happy birthday to you."

9. my friend, rosa, speaks spanish and i speak english.

10. my neighbor, julia, is going to be an exchange student in paris, france, next august.

End Marks

Every sentence must end with a punctuation mark. As you have been learning, a sentence may end with a period, a question mark, or an exclamation point.

- A period comes at the end of a sentence that tells something.

  Examples: I have a purple bicycle. Turn left at the corner.

- A question mark comes at the end of a sentence that asks a question.

  Examples: What color is your bicycle? Is that your house?

- An exclamation point comes at the end of a sentence that contains a strong feeling.

  Examples: Watch out for that car! What a wonderful surprise!

The following sentences need end marks. Think about which kind of end mark each sentence needs. Then write the correct punctuation mark at the end of each sentence.

1. I love my purple bicycle ☐

2. I saved enough money to buy it last year ☐

3. Would you like to try it ☐

4. My brother has a blue bicycle ☐

5. One time he crashed into me, and I fell off my bike ☐

6. Have you ever fallen off your bike ☐

7. Did you skin your knee ☐

8. I was so mad at my brother ☐

9. He told me he was sorry ☐

10. I'm so glad that my bike did not break ☐

11. Watch out for the glass in the road ☐

12. Don't ride your bike in the street ☐

13. Can you park a bike right here ☐

14. I have to go inside now ☐

15. Will I see you tomorrow ☐

Punctuation Rules

By now you are familiar with periods, question marks, and exclamation points. Here are some more punctuation tools you can use.

You should use a comma (**,**):
- to indicate a pause between adjectives, clauses, phrases, or combined sentences. **Examples:** My dad is a painter, and my mom is a musician. Even after our vacation, I still wanted to rest.
- to separate a city and a state. **Example:** Denver, Colorado
- between the day and year in a date. **Example:** May 20, 1949
- to separate three or more words or phrases in a list or series. **Examples:** I want to be an astronaut, a scientist, and a teacher. I like the colors blue, green, and red.
- after introductory words at the beginning of a sentence. **Example:** Yes, you can go.
- after the name of a person you are speaking to.
  Example: Jeremy, I see you.
- to indicate words that interrupt a sentence. **Example:** I, of course, couldn't sit still.
- to separate who is talking from a quotation. **Examples:** She asked, "What are you doing?" "I am not going to tell you," I said.

You should use an apostrophe (**'**):
- for contractions. **Examples:** it's, you've, I'm
- to indicate possession. **Examples:** David's umbrella, a plumber's tools

You should use a colon(**:**):
- to introduce a list. **Example:** Bring the following: pencils, paper, glue, and a ruler.
- to introduce a long quotation. Note that long quotes introduced by a colon are indented on each side and do not use quotation marks.
  Example: This morning the principal said: All students who are planning to attend Outdoor Education must come to an important meeting this evening at 7 o'clock. Be sure to bring your registration forms, deposit checks, and medical release forms.

You should use quotation marks (**" "**) at the beginning and end of a direct quote.
Example: Wanda said, "I want to go to the movies."

On a separate sheet of paper, write the story using correct punctuation.

It was a clear calm day on April 1 1995 I was a student at Oak Grove Elementary School My teacher Mrs. Griffon came into the classroom and smiled Suddenly Jeffrey jumped up and said Mrs. Griffon there's a spider crawling on your head Oh said Marisa where is the spider Mrs. Griffon pretended that she was afraid but only for a minute Then she yelled April fool We all laughed Then Mrs. Griffon explained how the first day of April is always April Fool s Day After we talked about it she told us to put our jackets away get out our reading books and take out some paper It was time for us to look up our spelling words But first she said she would read a story if we could quickly and quietly get ready for spelling All of us were ready except for Marisa Marisa where are you Mrs. Griffon asked Marisa said I m hiding from the spider

What Is a Subject?

All sentences have a subject. A subject tells who or what a sentence is about.

Example: Blake loves to paint.

    Who loves to paint? **Blake** loves to paint.

    Blake is the subject of the sentence.

First, ask yourself who or what the sentence is about. Then, underline the subject of the sentence. Finally, write the subject of the sentence on the line. The first one is done for you.

1. <u>Blake</u> has a paintbox.

    Who has a paintbox? Blake _____

2. The paintbox has three colors.

    What has three colors? _____

3. The colors are red, yellow, and blue.

    What are red, yellow, and blue?_____

4. Blake can make more colors.

    Who can make more colors? _____

5. Green is made by mixing together blue and yellow paints.

    What is made by mixing together blue and yellow paints? _____

6. Orange is made by mixing together yellow and red paints.

    What is made by mixing together yellow and red paints? _____

7. Blake loves to paint.

    Who loves to paint? _____

8. Blake's favorite color is blue.

    What is blue? _____

9. Mom hung up Blake's painting.

    Who hung up Blake's painting? _____

10. The painting is of a sailboat on the ocean.

    What is of a sailboat on the ocean?_____

Subject Practice

The subject is who or what the sentence is about. When an artist creates a painting of a vase full of colorful flowers, set upon a white cloth in front of a blue background, the subject of the painting is the vase of colorful flowers. The rest of the painting just gives more information about the vase of flowers, such as where they are and what kind of light is shining on them.

Example: Swimming is fun.

What is fun? **Swimming** is fun.

Swimming is the subject of the sentence.

First, ask yourself who or what the sentence is about. Then, underline the subject of the sentence. Finally, write the subject of the sentence on the line. The first one is done for you.

1. <u>Kids</u> love to swim at the pool and the beach.

   Who loves to swim at the pool and the beach? Kids _____

2. Baseball is a fun sport to play or watch.

   What is a fun sport to play or watch?_____

3. Swimming is a good way to cool off when it is hot.

   What is a good way to cool off when it is hot?_____

4. I like to eat ice cream in the summer.

   Who likes to eat ice cream in the summer?_____

5. Summertime is my favorite time of the year.

   What is your favorite time of the year? _____

6. In the summer, Jeremy likes to take a vacation.

   Who likes to take a vacation in the summer? _____

7. Mosquitoes are numerous in the summer.

   What are numerous in the summer? _____

8. My skin itches when I get a sunburn.

   What itches when you get a sunburn?_____

9. Every summer seashells wash up on the shore.

   What washes up on the shore every summer? _____

10. The summer is over, but it will be back next year.

    What is over but will be back next year? _____

Very Important Subjects

Now it is your turn to write some sentences using subjects. Choose eight subjects from the list in the box. On the lines provided at the bottom of the page, write a sentence using each of the subjects you have chosen. If you would prefer something more challenging than just writing sentences, try using the eight subjects you have chosen to write a story. Be sure all of your sentences fit together to tell the story. Another idea is to write the eight sentences using the subjects you have chosen. Then pick one or two of your sentences to write a story on a separate sheet of paper.

• Richard	• Aunt Wanda	• beach	• pizza	• space ship
• Lisa	• snakes	• jet plane	• movies	• camera
• Mario	• fish	• envelope	• giant	• night light
• backyard	• puppy	• crayons	• monster	• cowboy hat
• forest	• bees	• light bulb	• flowers	• book
• school	• rabbits	• library	• Ms. Brown	• chocolate
• first aid kit	• electric car	• truck	• ocean	• beach ball
• peanuts	• dog	• Officer Watts	• ice cream	• bowl of fruit
• basketball	• tiger	• staircase	• Mr. Willetts	• candy
• lifeguard	• zoo	• haunted house	• alien	• jacket

1. _____

_____

2. _____

_____

3. _____

_____

4. _____

_____

5. _____

_____

6. _____

_____

7. _____

_____

8. _____

_____

What is a Predicate?

Just as all sentences have a subject, they also have a predicate. The predicate tells us important things about the subject. It tells us what the subject does, has, or is.

Examples:

Tommy had a cold.
> What did Tommy have? Tommy **had a cold.**
> The predicate of the sentence is *had a cold.*

Felicia jumps into the lake.
> What does Felicia do? Felicia **jumps into the lake.**
> The predicate of the sentence is *jumps into the lake.*

The inner tube is leaking air.
> What is the inner tube doing? The inner tube **is leaking air.**
> The predicate of the sentence is *is leaking air.*

First, ask yourself what the subject does, has, or is. Then, circle the predicate of the sentence. The first one is done for you.

1. The water (is very cold.)
2. We jump into the water.
3. Luke splashes us.
4. Tonia is cold.
5. She gets out of the water.
6. Nick does a handstand underwater.
7. Everyone claps for him
8. The inner tube has a leak in it.
9. Luke throws the inner tube onto the shore.
10. Tonia sits on the inner tube.
11. The inner tube deflates with Tonia on it.
12. Everyone laughs with Tonia.
13. Tonia jumps into the water.
14. Luke swims as fast as he can.
15. Tonia races Luke.

What is Missing?

Here are some sentences that are missing subjects or predicates. Choose a subject or predicate from the box to complete each sentence. Then, on the line before each number, write a **P** if you added a predicate or an **S** if you added a subject to the sentence. The first one is done for you.

The following subjects and predicates may be used more than once.

My teacher	An ugly grasshopper	fell on my toe.
The mail carrier	The tree	is growling.
My kitten	has an attitude.	is singing in an opera.
has a cute little hat.	is crying.	is really an alien.
A ladybug	climbs on the furniture.	is covered in stripes.
Uncle Gerald	is lost in space.	was under the house.
My sister	Dinner	is as big as Australia.
A cute little baby	My bed	is a spy.
A suitcase	drove over the hills	The doctor
is very gross.	ran on the playground.	floats away.
is drooling.	snores.	is purple with polka dots.

_S_ 1. _____My Kitten_____ sat on the birthday cake.

_____ 2. _____ ate worms for breakfast.

_____ 3. Laurie _____ .

_____ 4. _____ slipped on a banana peel.

_____ 5. Mrs. Crabapple _____ .

_____ 6. _____ is a big, hairy beast.

_____ 7. A giant elephant _____ .

_____ 8. My little brother _____ .

_____ 9. The grizzly bear _____ .

_____ 10. _____ is very heavy.

_____ 11. _____ has the measles.

_____ 12. A jet plane _____ .

_____ 13. _____ is green.

_____ 14. My science book _____ .

_____ 15. _____ is growing blue fur.

Matching

Students may play the matching game by themselves or with partners.

Preparation: Reproduce pages 22 and 23, one copy for each student or pair of students. Cut out the subject and predicate strips. Glue them onto 3" x 5" (8 cm x 13 cm) index cards. Allow the glue to dry. Cut out the directions, and place a copy with each set of game cards.

Directions: Shuffle the cards and place them facedown in random order. Turn a card over and look at it. Turn another card over. If the two cards go together to make a complete sentence, keep them. If they do not make a complete sentence, turn both of them back over. If you are playing by yourself, try again. You win when you have made as many matched pairs as possible. If you are playing with someone else, let your partner take a turn. The winner is the player holding the greatest number of matched pairs. **Challenge:** At the end of the game, tell whether each card you have in your hand is a subject or a predicate.

Subject Cards

John	Mr. Samuel	Tara
the octopus	a refrigerator	the door
my ears	your hair	my big toe
Ms. Newsome	Lyle the Lizard	the tow truck
my pizza	your shoe	my bed
your brother	my candy bar	my dinner
your pencil	my homework	the class

Matching *(cont.)*

Subject Cards *(cont.)*

a swimming pool	the laughing rabbit	a spaceship
the ice cream cone	your nose	that old moldy brownie
the bathtub	my cat	Governor Mulroy

Predicate Cards

is asleep	had so much fun	likes me
needs to be washed	has a friend	has poison oak
is upside down	is blue	is in my pocket
is my favorite	ran in your yard	needs to be fed
is next on my list	is on my head	falls apart
is not a good idea	should be put away	twirls
runs down the street	itches	is ticklish
is delicious	hangs from the roof	can talk
is stuck to a tree	will sing	dances on the stage
went to Mars	should be eaten	is in my ear

The Verb is Superb!

Now you know what a predicate is. Did you notice that a predicate always has a verb? Verbs are very important.

- A verb can tell what the subject does. This is called an action verb.

  Example: Jacob runs home.

  What does Jacob do? **runs**

  The action verb is *runs.*

- A verb can also join the subject with another word or phrase by telling what the subject has or is. This is called a non-action verb.

  Example: Ruth has a sore throat.

  The non-action verb is *has.*

Fold along the dotted line shown below so you cannot see the Answer Key. Circle the verbs in the following sentences. Then, on the line before each number, write an **A** if you circled an action verb or an **N** if you circled a non-action verb. Use the Answer Key to check your answers. How many did you get right?

_____ 1. Marci sings in the choir.

_____ 2. Yoshi kicks the soccer ball.

_____ 3. Matt has the flu.

_____ 4. Leeann is really smart.

_____ 5. Mrs. Ross was my teacher.

_____ 6. The dog tipped over the trash can.

_____ 7. Next the dog jumped on Leticia.

_____ 8. Mr. Carter's shirt is dirty.

_____ 9. They walk to the store.

_____ 10. Toby washes his shirt.

Answer Key

1. A—sings	3. N—has	5. N—was	7. A—jumped	9. A—walk
2. A—kicks	4. N—is	6. A—tipped	8. N—is	10. A—washes

Take Action!

An action verb tells what the subject does. It shows action.

Examples: run, swing, jump, laugh, see, hit, leap

What are some of your favorite action verbs? Write them here: _____

_____

In the following paragraph, there are fifty action verbs. Can you find at least forty of them? When you find one, underline it and write it in the box at the bottom of the page.

In the morning, Benjamin woke up and jumped out of bed. He landed on his brother, Timothy, who was asleep in the bottom bunk. Timothy sat up and rubbed his eyes. He grumbled at Benjamin then fell back on his bed. Benjamin looked at Timothy for a long time. He wanted to see if Timothy was asleep. Then Benjamin ran to the corner and grabbed his horn. Benjamin blew into his horn and played some musical notes. He liked the way his horn sounded. But he heard another sound. He stopped and listened. A moaning sound came from Timothy. Benjamin didn't like that sound. He grabbed his horn and ran out the door. He sat on the front lawn and played some more music. The notes floated in the air. He felt happy until he heard another sound. He stopped and listened. A groaning sound came from his next door neighbor. Benjamin ran into the backyard. He played his horn some more. He liked the notes. Then he heard another sound. It was his mother. She called his name again. He went inside. His mother took his horn and put it away. Then she put Benjamin back in his bed. She told him it was too early to get up. Benjamin's mother went back to bed, too. Benjamin tried to imagine the sounds of his horn. Suddenly, he heard another sound. He stopped and listened. Timothy snored again and again. Benjamin moaned. He stuck his fingers in his ears, but he still heard Timothy. So he covered his ears with his pillow. Soon he fell fast asleep.

_____

_____

_____

_____

_____

_____

_____

_____

_____

Take a Break!

You have learned that all sentences have verbs. A verb can be a word that tells what a subject does. When a verb tells what a subject does, it is called an action verb. However, a verb can also be a word that tells us what the subject *has* or *is*. When a verb describes what a subject *has* or i*s*, it is called a non-action verb.

Examples:

My friend **has** a dog. The non-action verb is *has*.

The dog **is** nice. The non-action verb is *is*.

We **were** on the boat with the dog. The non-action verb is *were*.

Find the non-action verbs in the following sentences. Underline them in the sentences. Then write them on the lines at the bottom of the page. The first one is done for you.

1. My sister <u>has</u> a turtle.
2. The turtle is very small.
3. I have a cat.
4. My cat was very sleepy.
5. My brothers had a wagon.
6. They are always busy.
7. The turtle and the cat were in the wagon.
8. My brothers are in trouble.
9. The cat was with my brothers.
10. My sister is older than my brother.

1. _____ has _____   6. _____

2. _____   7. _____

3. _____   8. _____

4. _____   9. _____

5. _____   10. _____

We're Here to Help!

Some non-action verbs help action verbs do their work. They work together in a sentence, like a team. These non-action verbs are called helping verbs.

Example: People **can travel** in many ways.

    The non-action helping verb is *can*.

    The action verb is *travel*.

    The complete verb is *can travel*.

Find the helping and action verbs in sentences shown below. Use the following list of verbs to help you. Then fill in the chart at the bottom of the page by writing the helping and action verbs from the sentences.

Helping Verbs: am   is   has   are   were   has   have   had   can   will

Action Verbs: drink ridden pushed driven move pulled going ride seen go

1. Jimmy will ride his bicycle.
2. An elephant is ridden in India.
3. The scooters were pushed by the children.
4. An airplane can move quickly.
5. Amy has driven a bus.
6. Sled dogs have pulled the children across the snow.
7. I have seen a bear.
8. You will go to a birthday party.
9. Henry is going to eat all the cake.
10. We will drink all the punch.

Helping Verbs

1. _____
2. _____
3. _____
4. _____
5. _____
6. _____
7. _____
8. _____
9. _____
10. _____

Action Verbs

1. _____
2. _____
3. _____
4. _____
5. _____
6. _____
7. _____
8. _____
9. _____
10. _____

Just One or More?

Subjects and verbs are very important parts of a sentence. They need to get along well. If they do not agree with each other, your sentence will not sound right. It is important that they agree in number. A singular subject tells about one person, place, or thing. It needs a singular verb. A plural subject tells about more than one person, place, or thing. It needs a plural verb.

Example:

Singular Subjects		Plural Subjects	
dress	rabbit	dresses	rabbits
car	Michael	cars	Michael and Jason
boy	house	boys	houses
Singular Verbs		**Plural Verbs**	
has	jumps	have	hop
is	hops	run	sing
runs	sings	jump	are

In the following sentences, circle the correct verb. On the line before each number, write an **S** if you circled a singular verb or a **P** if you circled a plural verb.

_____ 1. The dress (has, have) a big bow in back.

_____ 2. These cars (runs, run) funny.

_____ 3. The boys (jumps, jump) from the tree.

_____ 4. The rabbit (hops, hop) around the yard.

_____ 5. Michael and Jason (sing, sings) this morning.

_____ 6. My house (are, is) yellow and white.

_____ 7. All the houses on our street (are, is) one story.

_____ 8. Michael (hop, hops) on one foot.

_____ 9. My old toy car (are, is) rusty.

_____ 10. Our rabbit (has, have) a large cage.

Now write your own sentences on the lines below. Write one sentence with a singular subject and verb and another sentence with a plural subject and verb. Make your sentences as interesting as you can.

1. Singular: _____

2. Plural: _____

What's That You Say?

You already know about ending sentences with periods, question marks, and exclamation points. Sentences with these different endings have different names. Use the information below and on page 30 to learn about the four kinds of sentences.

- Sentences that make statements end with periods. They are called **declarative sentences.**

  Examples: Sunday is my grandma's birthday. It will rain tomorrow.
- Sentences that ask questions end with question marks. They are called **interrogative sentences.**

  Examples: Is this seat taken? Can I play? Do you want this? Where are you going?
- Sentences that express strong emotion end with exclamation points. These are called **exclamatory sentences**.

  Examples: We're going to Disney World! Tommy's cat won first prize at the fair!
- Sentences that make requests end with periods. Sentences that give commands or make strong or urgent requests end with exclamation points. All of these types of sentences are called **imperative sentences.**

  Examples: Put the book on the shelf. Watch out! Don't put those peas on your head!
- It might seem like an imperative sentence does not have a subject. You cannot see it in the sentence, but it is there. The subject is YOU. Test it for yourself. When someone says to you, "Please put the book on the shelf," the subject *you* is not in the sentence. However, you know that the person is speaking to you. The person could say, "You, please put the book on the shelf." You can add the subject *you* to the beginning of any imperative sentence.

  Example: (*You*) Wash the dishes.

Decide whether the following sentences are imperatives or declaratives. On the line before each number, write an **I** if it is an imperative sentence or a **D** if it is a declarative sentence.

_____ 1. The top fell off my new toy soldier.   _____ 6. I can't find my shoes.

_____ 2. Put me down, please.   _____ 7. Give me my hat.

_____ 3. Open your science books.   _____ 8. Marie, I will tickle you.

_____ 4. My dog ate my homework.   _____ 9. Stop!

_____ 5. Take out the trash now!   _____ 10. I warned you not to do that.

What's That You Say? *(cont.)*

Sentences that end with question marks are always **interrogatives.** Interrogative sentences ask questions. Another way to tell if a sentence is an interrogative is to ask yourself, "Does the main verb come before the subject?" If the main verb comes before the subject, it is an interrogative sentence.

Write five questions that you would like to ask your teacher.

1. _____
   _____

2. _____
   _____

3. _____
   _____

4. _____
   _____

5. _____
   _____

Great job! You have written five interrogative sentences.

Put a period at the end of each declarative sentence or imperative sentence that makes a request. Put an exclamation point at the end of each exclamatory sentence or imperative sentence that gives a command or makes a strong or urgent request .

1. I am very tired ☐
2. Let's sit down here ☐
3. What a wonderful idea ☐
4. Ouch ☐
5. Watch where you throw that ball ☐
6. Well, then, let's have some lunch ☐
7. The sandwich is for you ☐
8. That lasagne is very hot ☐
9. I didn't think you wanted lasagna ☐
10. Sue would like a hamburger, please ☐
11. Bob, you don't have to get so upset ☐
12. This sandwich tastes good ☐
13. I love roast beef ☐
14. Take your brother to the park ☐

Can You Handle This?

You have probably noticed that some sentences could be either exclamatory or declarative. The more writing you do, the more you will notice that you are in control. You, as the writer, determine whether or not sentences will express strong feelings. The way you punctuate affects the meaning as shown in the following examples.

Examples:

1. I got a B on the test!

2. I got a B on the test.

In the first sentence, the student is very happy and excited about earning a B. In the second sentence, the student is just telling someone that he or she earned a B.

Correct the paragraph shown below. You will need to remember everything that you have learned about complete sentences, capitalization, and punctuation. When you have finished correcting the paragraph, proofread it to avoid any careless errors. You may wish to change some of your answers. Revise the paragraph, and read it one more time. After you have rechecked your answers, use the back of this paper to write a new paragraph that includes as many declarative, interrogative, imperative, and exclamatory sentences as you can. This is your chance to be creative and use your imagination.

i went to the store because i needed to get something for lunch my stomach was growling so much that a little boy sitting in a shopping cart could hear it Mom, he said, he has a rumbly tumbly Shush said his mother i turned to the little boy and asked i have a what A rumbly tumbly he said and smiled shyly. A rumbly tumbly, a rumbly tumbly i said over and over again the little boy started to giggle and i was even hungrier than before yikes i said to the little boy. i have to get something to eat before my rumbly tumbly tumbles the little boy stopped giggling, pointed his finger at me, and said, go get something to eat right now before your rumbly tumbly tumbles okay i said as i rushed down the aisle toward the apples and bananas.

My Complements to This Sentence!

When you eat at a nice restaurant, the food tastes good because the chef does not cook just plain food. The chef makes the food with lots of extras, such as herbs and spices. If you tasted the plain food, you would say, "This is good." If you tasted the food with herbs and spices added, you would say, "This is delicious!"

The same is true with sentences. You can add information to a plain sentence to make it more interesting. As you have learned, every predicate has a verb. Sometimes a predicate has extra words that are called complements. A complement is a word or group of words that completes the predicate. It adds more information to a sentence.

Examples:

1. Jimmy jumps.

    Jimmy jumps on me. The complement is *on me.*

2. I walked.

    I walked into the post. The complement is *into the post.*

Now it is your turn. Use your imagination to add some complements to the following phrases and sentences. Remember that a complement is a word or group of words that adds extra information to the predicate.

1. The race car driver sped _____

2. My sister screamed _____

3. The monster climbed _____

4. I saw a fat giraffe _____

5. An alien space craft landed _____

6. I want to run _____

7. Don't tell _____

8. My baby brother threw _____

9. A ton of broccoli fell _____

10. A big, purple bird flew _____

11. An ugly spider is crawling _____

12. Shameka and Patty ran _____

13. I don't want to see _____

14. The shooting star burst _____

15. Hector closed _____

Enchanted Enhancements

Sometimes a simple, complete sentence is all that is needed. However, at other times it is a good idea to give more details.

Example:

Lorna saw a dog. When you read this sentence, you probably imagine some kind of dog. If all of your classmates drew pictures of the dog, each one would be very different.

Lorna saw a monstrous, hairy dog, with legs that were three-feet long, and it drooled as it trotted directly toward her! When you read this sentence, you have a much better idea of what the dog looked like. Descriptive language and additional information about the subject is very useful and makes the sentence more interesting.

A word that helps describe something is an **adjective**. There are three types of adjectives.

- **Demonstrative Adjectives:** These point out. They answer the question, "Which one(s)?" Examples: *this, that, these, those — I like this dress. Those cookies look delicious.*

- **Common Adjectives:** These describe the subject in a general way. They answer the question, "*What kind of?*" or "*How many?*" Examples: *soft, warm, six, blue, sunny, tired, tall. The building is tall. The kitten is soft.*

- **Proper Adjectives:** These are made from proper nouns and are always capitalized. They answer the question, "What kind of?" Examples: *Irish, Martian, African American, Native American, Elizabethan — I love French cheese! There are many Japanese cars.*

In the following sentences, circle the adjectives. Then, on the lines, write the questions (What kind of? How many? Which one?) that the adjectives answer.

1. I don't like this sandwich. _____

2. The old man came to the door. _____

3. Most French students speak English. _____

4. We're learning a Scottish dance tomorrow. _____

5. The yellow flowers are wilting. _____

6. I have three brothers. _____

7. For dinner tonight, they're serving a delicious spinach casserole. _____

8. Give me your dollar, and I'll give you my comic book. _____

9. Tim doesn't want that soft pear. _____

10. Watch out for the mean dog down the street. _____

11. My clueless brother threw away my homework. _____

12. Those black shoes are too small. _____

Enchanted Enhancements *(cont.)*

Now it is your turn to enhance the sentences in the following story. Fill in the blanks with descriptive words or phrases. You may use demonstrative adjectives (such as this, that, these, and those), common adjectives (such as birthday, large, frozen, lovely, three), and proper adjectives (such as British, German, and Jurassic). You may also wish to use descriptive phrases (such as weather-beaten or pocket-sized). Have fun with this activity, but remember to try for interesting images with descriptive language rather than choosing words or phrases that will make the sentences sound silly.

It was my _____ birthday so I ran home from school. When I got to my _____ house it looked like no one was home. "Hello!" I shouted. "Where is my _____ family? Your _____ son and brother is home now!" No one answered. I went to our _____ kitchen to see if there was a note. No note. Not even a _____ note. I went into the _____ room and turned on the _____ television. There was a _____ show on. I turned the television off. I went back into the kitchen to get something to eat. "I want something that's _____ to eat," I said to myself. I saw yogurt but it was pineapple flavored. "I don't want _____ yogurt. I want _____ yogurt," I said, grabbing a _____ yogurt. I sat down to eat the _____ yogurt. Then I looked for something else. I found _____ candy. I was just about to eat it when the _____ telephone rang. "Hello?" It was my _____ mom. She told me she would be home soon, but needed me to go into the _____ basement to get a _____ chicken from the _____ freezer. "Okay," I said. Then I ate some _____ candy.

The telephone rang again. "Honey," my mom said, "please get the _____ chicken from the basement now!"

"Okay!" I said again. As I walked toward the _____ basement stairs I started wondering how she knew I hadn't gone down to the basement yet. I opened the _____ door. I slowly crept down the _____ steps into the _____ basement. I was getting the creeps. How did she know? Why was it so dark? The _____ stairs made creaking noises. Finally, I got to the bottom and waved my hand around to try to find the _____ light switch. I felt some _____ cobwebs and shrieked just a little. Just then, the _____ lights came on and I heard _____ voices screaming, "Happy Birthday!" I nearly ran all the way back up the _____ steps. My heart was pounding so hard I thought it would break right through my _____ chest! I saw the _____ basement was full of _____ people. They were holding _____ balloons and _____ gifts. Everyone I knew was there— my _____ mom, my _____ Aunt Amelia, my _____ sister Lindsay, all our _____ neighbors and all of my _____ friends.

So _____ is where everyone was, and _____ was how my _____ mom knew I hadn't come downstairs yet. The _____ chicken, I just remembered! I went to the _____ freezer and opened the door to grab a _____ chicken. Everyone stared at me. Then they all started to laugh. "No, honey," my mom said, "we don't need a chicken after all. Tonight we're having _____ pizza and _____ birthday cake with _____ candles!" We went upstairs and had a party!

Word Muncher

A word muncher is a kind of monster that only eats parts of sentences. You can tell that a word muncher has been here because these sentences are full of holes. See if you can save these sentences by filling in the missing subjects or predicates.

1. The word muncher _____

    _____

2. _____ (was, were) very hungry.

3. _____ jumped up and down on my bed.

4. Twelve gorillas _____

    _____

5. _____ fell into the trunk of my neighbor's car.

6. A tiny little dancer _____

    _____

7. _____ sat on a mushroom.

8. A large box of soap _____

    _____

9. My Aunt Gertrude _____

    _____

10. _____ (is, are) sloshing around in my pocket.

11. _____ (is, are) tumbling down the front steps.

12. My friend, Tiffany, _____

    _____

13. _____ bit my ear!

14. _____ escaped from (his, her, their, its) cage.

15. Your elbow _____

    _____

Crazy, Mixed-Up Sentences

Follow the directions on pages 36-38 to make and play this game. To make the Subject Cards, reproduce this page on red cardstock or sturdy paper, or glue it onto red construction paper. Cut apart the cards. Then make the Verb Cards (page 37) and the Complement Cards (page 38).

My teacher	A big green monster	My grandmother	A little baby
An alien from Mars	A koala bear	A humpback whale	A slimy creature
A dog as big as a horse	An orange grasshopper	A cute little boy	The trash collector
A hairy caterpillar	A large, blue refrigerator	A rock star	A giant raccoon

Crazy, Mixed-Up Sentences *(cont.)*

To make the Verb Cards, reproduce this page on blue cardstock or sturdy paper, or glue it onto blue construction paper. Cut apart the cards. Then make the Complement Cards (page 38). Finally, show students how to play the game using the directions on page 38.

leaps	growls	roars	giggles
sits	slithers	swims	sings
rolls	crawls	flies	eats
snores	cries	somersaults	slips

Crazy, Mixed-Up Sentences *(cont.)*

To make the Complement Cards, reproduce this page on orange cardstock or sturdy paper, or glue it onto orange construction paper. Cut apart the cards. Then have students follow these directions: Shuffle each set of cards. Place the sets of cards facedown in stacks. Choose one red, one blue, and one orange card. Use the three cards to make a sentence. Continue making sentences until you find one that you like. Write that sentence, and use it to write a story.

on my head.	around the world.	in a large vat of peanut butter.	with my dad.
in the forest.	at the airport.	behind the garage.	under the car.
all the time.	at our house.	in the bathtub.	in the air.
through the forest.	on top of a mountain	in the classroom.	on a piece of paper.

Sentence Construction Teams

Reproduce the sentence strips shown on this page and pages 40 and 41. Cut along the dashed lines. Then fold along the solid lines, accordion style. Assign partners or allow students to choose their own. Give several folded strips and an envelope to each team. The first player looks at the subject. If that space is blank, she or he writes a subject. If it is already filled in, she or he turns to the next fold and writes a verb. Next, the first player folds the strip so her or his partner can only see the space that is still blank. The partner fills in the blank without seeing the rest of the sentence and places the strip in the envelope. Teams continue to play until time is up or they run out of strips. Allow time for students to read their sentence strips to the class.

Extension: Divide the class into groups of three. Provide blank sentence strips. Tell students that each group member should write a different part of the sentence without looking at what the others have written.

Subject The talking horse	**Verb**	**Complement**
Subject	**Verb** climbs	**Complement**
Subject	**Verb**	**Complement** in and out of the bathtub.
Subject	**Verb** crashed	**Complement**
Subject A fuzzy monster	**Verb**	**Complement**
Subject	**Verb** slinks	**Complement**
Subject	**Verb**	**Complement** with a loud bang.
Subject An orange bug	**Verb**	**Complement**

Sentence Construction Teams *(cont.)*

Follow the directions on page 39 to make and play this game.

Subject The car	**Verb**	**Complement**
Subject My little brother	**Verb**	**Complement**
Subject	**Verb** flew	**Complement**
Subject	**Verb**	**Complement** in outer space.
Subject My shoe	**Verb**	**Complement**
Subject	**Verb**	**Complement** in the bathroom.
Subject	**Verb** is snoring	**Complement**
Subject A scary bear	**Verb**	**Complement**
Subject	**Verb**	**Complement** on my foot.
Subject	**Verb** ate	**Complement**
Subject	**Verb**	**Complement** on my head.

40

Sentence Construction Teams *(cont.)*

Follow the directions on page 39 to make and play this game.

Subject	Verb	Complement
Subject A spider	**Verb**	**Complement**
Subject	**Verb** shiver	**Complement**
Subject My sister	**Verb**	**Complement**
Subject	**Verb**	**Complement** down the stairs.
Subject	**Verb** stumbled	**Complement**
Subject	**Verb** tickled	**Complement**
Subject	**Verb**	**Complement** in my ice cream.
Subject The haunted house	**Verb**	**Complement**
Subject	**Verb** is dancing	**Complement**
Subject	**Verb**	**Complement** into my pocket.
Subject A sticky lollipop	**Verb**	**Complement**

 #2326 How to Write a Sentence

Sentence Maze

What is this girl going to do today? Find out by making a sentence as you go through the maze.

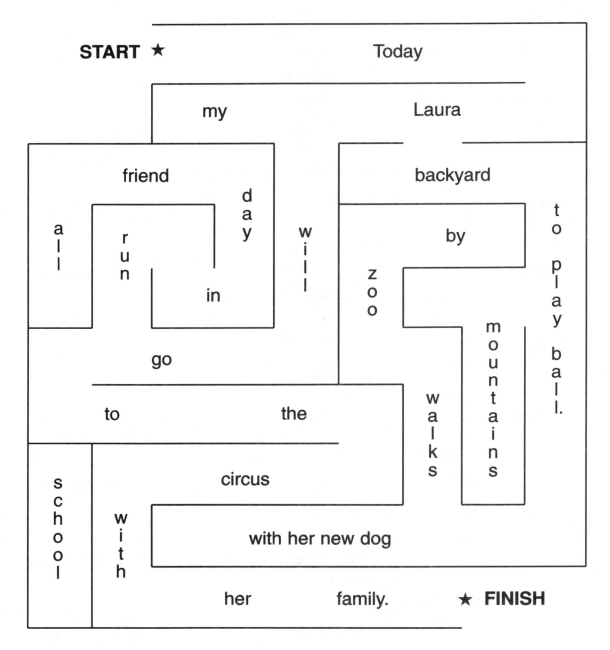

Now write the sentence here.

_____

_____

Sentence Rummy

Reproduce and cut out the cards shown below and on page 44, one set for each pair of students. Students play this card game like Rummy. Deal seven cards to each player and place the remainder of the deck facedown. Players try to make sentences using their cards. The words *a* or *the* may be added before any noun when making the sentence. Add capital letters and periods as needed. One point is earned for each card used in the sentence.

Examples:

[A clumsy] teacher tumbled [into the mud] yesterday. = 1 + 1 + 1 + 1 + 1 = 5 points

[*The* teacher] tumbled. = 1 + 1 = 2 points

Cards may be held back for strategic purposes. However, there is a risk in doing so. After the initial sentences are made with the cards both players have been dealt, player 1 asks player 2 for a card, according to its use such as noun, verb, adverb, complement or adjective. If player 2 has any cards of that type, he/she must give one of them to player 1. If player 2 does not have any of that type of card, player 1 draws from the deck. The winner is the player with the most points after all the cards in the deck have been drawn.

away from school *(complement)*	the silly *(adjective)*
A hungry *(adjective)*	A clumsy *(adjective)*
hippopotamus *(noun)*	teacher *(noun)*
galloped *(verb)*	tumbled *(verb)*
noisily *(adverb)*	awkwardly *(adverb)*
into the grocery store *(complement)*	into the mud *(complement)*
sentence *(noun)*	yesterday *(adverb)*
one *(adverb)*	slides *(verb)*

Sentence Rummy *(cont.)*

Follow the directions on page 43 to make and play this game. In addition to the Rummy game (page 43), you may wish to have students play Solitaire with the cards to build their sentence-making skills. As another alternative, pairs of students may pool their cards so four can play Rummy.

A gorgeous *(adjective)*	A sleepy *(adjective)*
A mischievous *(adjective)*	A studious *(adjective)*
baby *(noun)*	mountain goat *(noun)*
biker *(noun)*	parakeet *(noun)*
sang *(verb)*	jumped *(verb)*
crawled *(verb)*	danced *(verb)*
effortlessly *(adverb)*	cautiously *(adverb)*
quickly *(adverb)*	wildly *(adverb)*
around the park *(complement)*	over the TV set *(complement)*
behind me *(complement)*	toward my mother *(complement)*
skipped *(verb)*	coach *(noun)*
crocodile *(noun)*	sneezed *(verb)*

Award

Reproduce this award on brightly colored paper or cardstock. Fill it in and cut it out. You may wish to use scissors that cut with a fancy edge, such as pinking shears.

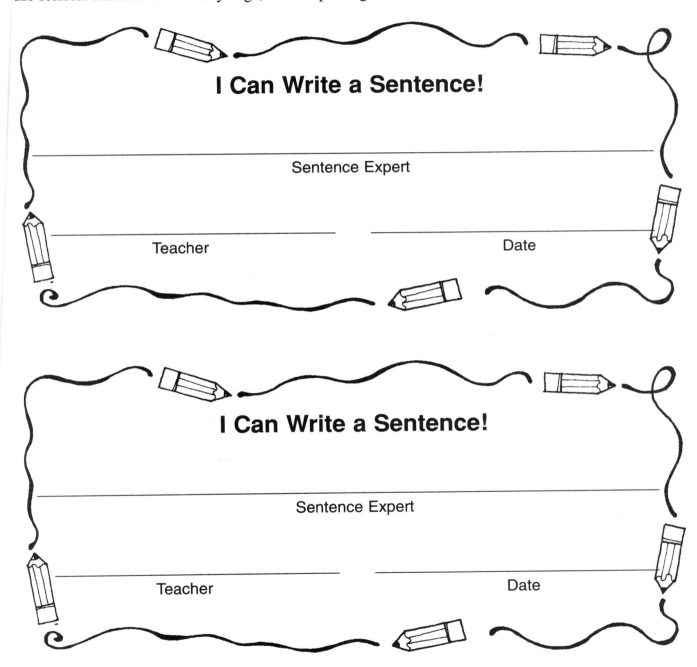

I Can Write a Sentence!

_____

Sentence Expert

_____ _____

Teacher   Date

I Can Write a Sentence!

_____

Sentence Expert

_____ _____

Teacher   Date

Answer Ke[y]

Page 6

The following sentences should be circled: 2, 5, 7, 9, 10, 14, 15.

Page 7

The following answers may appear in any order.

1. I'm going swimming after school!
2. Chris opens the door.
3. Will we go to the store tomorrow?
4. My iguana ate my homework.
5. Juanita helps me.
6. Can you come with me?
7. Maria dances every day.
8. I have a cat.
9. That bicycle looks brand new!
10. Do you like candy?

Page 8

1. Tuesday is the day we go to the library.
2. Who is your teacher?
3. The students in my class were reading.
4. What a wonderful day it is!
5. Jordan, come play with us. OR Jordan, come play with us!
6. Watch out, Michelle!
7. Do you like math?
8. I will paint today.
9. What time is lunch?
10. I got a sticker. OR I got a sticker!

Page 9

Answers will vary. Accept all correctly written sentences.

Page 10

1. My books are on the table. My math book is on top.
2. They were closing the store. It was time to go home.
3. Watch out for the slippery ice! You could fall and hurt yourself.
4. I got a new blue dress. The blue shoes match perfectly.
5. My brother made the team!

Will I be able to play [ ] some day?

6. I like to go camping. [ ] time we went, we sa[ ]
7. My teacher was not [ ] We had a substitute.
8. I don't like lima be[ ] want mashed potatoes.
9. Can you spend the night at my house? We can have pizza for dinner.
10. My dog has fleas. We had to get her some special medicine.

Page 11

(1) Every day the ice cream truck comes down our street.
(2) It comes after school and in the summer.
(3) When I hear the music playing, I run outside. (4) Sometimes I get to buy some ice cream. (5) Do you like ice cream?
(6) My sister does not like ice cream. (7) I think that is crazy.
(8) How can someone not like ice cream? (9) It is nice to eat on a hot summer day. (10) I think I like chocolate best of all!

Page 12

Answers will vary. Accept all correctly written sentences.

Page 13

1. Bruce has many things in his room.
2. Answers will vary. Accept all correctly written sentences.
3. Is there a box of toys under the bed?
4. A rug is in front of the closet.
5. Answers will vary. Accept all correctly written sentences.
6. I can see trees from my window.
7. Answers will vary. Accept all correctly written sentences.
8. Answers will vary. Accept all correctly written sentences.

2. **My** family wi[ ] **Disneyland** in **July.**
3. **I** am reading *Old Yeller* this week.
4. **My** sister, **Sarah,** says her favorite subject is **Spanish.**
5. **On Wednesday,** we will celebrate **Groundhog Day.**
6. **My** brother said that **Mom** was a cheerleader at **Roosevelt High School.**
7. **In August,** we're going to visit **Aunt Margaret** in **San Francisco, California.**
8. **Benjie,** my little brother, had a birthday and we sang, "**Happy Birthday to You!**"
9. **My** friend, **Rosa,** speaks **Spanish** and **I** speak **English.**
10. **My** neighbor, **Julia,** is going to be an exchange student in **Paris, France,** next **August.**

Page 15

1. I love my purple bicycle!
2. I saved enough money to buy it last year. OR I saved enough money to buy it last year!
3. Would you like to try it?
4. My brother has a blue bicycle.
5. One time he crashed into me, and I fell off my bike.
6. Have you ever fallen off your bike?
7. Did you skin your knee?
8. I was so mad at my brother!
9. He told me he was sorry.
10. I'm so glad that my bike did not break OR I'm so glad that my bike did not break!

Answer Key (cont.)

Page 15 (cont.)
11. Watch out for the glass in the road!
12. Don't ride your bike in the street! OR Don't ride your bike in the street.
13. Can you park a bike right here?
14. I have to go inside now.
15. Will I see you tomorrow?

Page 16
The following can be written in paragraph form or as individual sentences.

It was a clear, calm day on April 1, 1995. I was a student at Oak Grove Elementary School. My teacher, Mrs. Griffon, came into the classroom and smiled.

Suddenly, Jeffrey jumped up and said, "Mrs. Griffon, there's a spider crawling on your head!"

"Oh," said Marisa, "where is the spider?"

Mrs. Griffon pretended that she was afraid, but only for a minute. Then she yelled, "April fool!" We all laughed. Then Mrs. Griffon explained how the first day of April is always April Fool's Day. After we talked about it, she told us to put our jackets away, get out our reading books, and take out some paper. It was time for us to look up our spelling words. But first, she said she would read a story if we could quickly and quietly get ready for spelling.

All of us were ready except for Marisa. "Marisa, where are you?" Mrs. Griffon asked.

Marisa said, "I'm hiding from the spider."

Page 17
The following answers should be underlined in the sentences and written in response to the questions.
1. Blake

2. the paintbox
3. the colors
4. Blake
5. green
6. orange
7. Blake's favorite color
8. Blake
9. Mom
10. the painting

Page 18
The following answers should be underlined in the sentences and written in response to the questions.
1. kids
2. baseball
3. swimming
4. I
5. summertime
6. Jeremy
7. mosquitoes
8. my skin
9. seashells
10. summer

Page 19
Answers will vary. Accept all correctly written sentences.

Page 20
The following predicates should be circled.
1. is very cold
2. jump into the water
3. splashes us
4. is cold
5. gets out of the water
6. does a handstand underwater
7. claps for him
8. has a leak in it
9. throws the inner tube onto the shore
10. sits on the inner tube
11. deflates with Tonia on it
12. laughs with Tonia
13. jumps into the water
14. swims as fast as he can
15. races Luke

Page 21
Subject and predicate choices will vary. Check to be sure students have picked an appropriate choice for each sentence.
1. S
2. S
3. P
4. S
5. P
6. S
7. P
8. P
9. P
10. S
11. S
12. P
13. S
14. P
15. S

Page 25
woke, jumped, landed, sat, rubbed, grumbled, fell, looked, wanted, ran, grabbed, blew, played, liked, heard, stopped, listened, came, like, grabbed, ran, sat, played, floated, felt, heard, stopped, listened, came, ran, played, liked, heard, called, went, took, put, put, told, went, tried, heard, stopped, listened, snored, moaned, stuck, heard, covered, fell

Page 26
The following non-action verbs should be underlined in the sentences and written on the lines at the bottom of the page.
1. has
2. is
3. have
4. was
5. had

Page 26 (cont.)
6. are
7. were
8. are
9. was
10. is

Answer Key (cont.)

Page 27

Helping Verbs
1. will
2. is
3. were
4. can
5. has
6. have
7. have
8. will
9. is
10. will

Action Verbs
1. ride
2. ridden
3. pushed
4. move
5. driven
6. pulled
7. seen
8. go
9. going
10. drink

Page 28
1. S—has
2. P—run
3. P—jump
4. S—hops
5. P—sing
6. S—is
7. P—are
8. S—hops
9. S—is
10. S—has

1. and 2. Answers will vary. Accept all correctly written sentences. The first sentence should have a singular subject and verb. The second sentence should have a plural subject and verb.

Page 29
1. D
2. I
3. I
4. D
5. I
6. D
7. I
8. D
9. I
10. D

Page 30
1.-5. Answers will vary. Accept all correctly written questions.
1. I am very tired.
2. Let's sit down here.
3. What a wonderful idea!
4. Ouch!
5. Watch where you throw that ball!
6. Well, then, let's have some lunch.
7. The sandwich is for you.
8. That lasagna is very hot! OR That lasagna is very hot.
9. I didn't think you wanted lasagna.
10. Sue would like a hamburger, please.
11. Bob, you don't have to get so upset! OR Bob, you don't have to get so upset.
12. This sandwich tastes good.
13. I love roast beef! OR I love roast beef.
14. Take your brother to the park.

Page 31
Students may show the following answer in paragraph form or as individual sentences. Some ending punctuation may vary.
I went to the store because I needed to get something for lunch. My stomach was growling so much that a little boy sitting in a shopping cart could hear it. "Mom," he said, "he has a rumbly tumbly!"
"Shush," said his mother.
I turned to the little boy and asked, "I have a what?"
"A rumbly tumbly," he said and smiled shyly.
"A rumbly tumbly, a rumbly tumbly," I said over and over again. The little boy started to giggle, and I was even hungrier than before. "Yikes!" I said to the little boy. "I have to get something to eat before my rumbly tumbly tumbles!"
The little boy stopped giggling, pointed his finger at me, and said, "Go get something to eat right now before your rumbly tumbly tumbles!"
"Okay!" I said as I rushed down the aisle toward the apples and bananas.

Page 32
Answers will vary. Accept all correctly written complements.

Page 33
The adjectives should be circled.
1. this (Which one?)
2. old (What kind of?)
3. French (What kind of?)
4. Scottish (What kind of?)
5. yellow (What kind of?)
6. three (How many?)
7. delicious, spinach (What kind of?)
8. comic (What kind of?)
9. that (Which one?); soft (What kind of?)
10. mean (What kind of?)
11. clueless (What kind of?)
12. Those (Which ones?); black (What kind of?)

Page 34
Answers will vary. Accept all appropriate descriptive words and phrases.

Page 35
Answers will vary. Accept all appropriate subjects and predicates.

Page 42
Today Laura will go to the circus with her family.